The Kingdom of Darkness

Father Joseph Brennan

Acadian House
PUBLISHING
LAFAYETTE, LOUISIANA

Published by:
ACADIAN HOUSE PUBLISHING
Lafayette, Louisiana

ISBN: 0-925417-01-7

Printed in the United States of America

PREFACE

Funny how important people make first impressions. Such was the case 24 years ago when I first met a tall, gangly, Irish-American Catholic priest by the name of Joe Brennan in Lafayette, Louisiana.

I was a young reporter transitioning from newspaper to television, and I had the occasion to interview him. I don't recall the topic, but I do remember how precise and to the point he was, and that made choosing a sound bite very easy in the editing room. I also remember his quick wit and broad smile.

Life's roadmap led me to New Orleans and WWL Television, and I lost track of Brennan. Twenty-four years, sixteen thousand newscasts, and just about as many stories later, our paths crossed once again. Unlike our first intersection, we would travel the same difficult road together for a while. My monthly investigative "Journal," a one-hour program which goes on the air the first Sunday of each month, was looking into Satanism. Almost every inquiry about the subject led me to Brennan's doorstep.

After some convincing, the reluctant Brennan agreed to an interview. As the days turned into weeks and those into months, I became privy to an underworld of demented souls whose behavior in worshiping Satan opened a window on what hell must surely be like. Brennan cautioned me from the beginning that I would come under attack and that "once you uncork the bottle" there would be no turning back. He spoke from years of research and experience.

After two hour-long reports on the subject, I knew exactly what he was trying to warn me of. The attack by evil persons was furious, both politically and in print. I believe that my reputation and work survived.

I am now back to reporting other subjects. However, seldom does a day go by that I do not receive a call from a reporter somewhere in the country, wanting to know more about Satanism. Video tapes of those two segments that Brennan and I worked on are slowly making their way across the land — and people are believing.

If the reporters writing and broadcasting those stories learn their subject well, they will let their audiences and readers know that Father Joe Brennan was the point man in this escalating battle with Satan. This reporter found him to be a pit bull in defense of the helpless and a gentle old Saint Bernard with those who were so savagely abused.

The Bible says that Saint Michael, the Archangel, was chosen by God to battle Satan. Brennan would surely bring a smile to Saint Michael's face.

—BILL ELDER
New Orleans, La.

December 9, 1988

Reverend Joseph F. Brennan
Pastor
Post Office Drawer 90307
Lafayette, Louisiana 70509

Dear Father Brennan,

I wish to commend you for all of the assistance you have so generously rendered to the Archdiocese of New Orleans in conducting seminars for the priests of this area. You have given freely of your time and talents for the benefit of the people of God of this Archdiocese, for which I am deeply indebted to you. You have conducted the seminars with professional skill to the encouragement and inspiration of those who are in need of such instruction, as well as to those who will advise others in the future.

May God continue to abundantly bless you for your generous gifts to Him.

With cordial best wishes, renewed appreciation, and my prayers during this holy Christmas season, I remain,

Sincerely yours in Christ,

Archbishop of New Orleans

PMH:emk

October 3, 1988

The Reverend Joseph F. Brennan
St. Genevieve Church
Post Office Box 90307
Lafayette, Louisiana 70509

Dear Father Brennan:

It is good of you to share your experience and knowledge of the occult and satanic presence with your readers. It is my hope that your insights will be of assistance to those who must deal with these phenomena in modern society.

With every best wish, I remain

Sincerely in our Divine Savior,

†Gerard L. Frey
Bishop of Lafayette

GLF:lm

FOREWORD

This book is an effort to expose the Satanic underworld for what it is and to offer some advice to parents and children on how to keep the influence of the devil out of their lives.

The book is based on my experience as a counselor of ritualistically abused children and of others whose lives have been adversely affected by the hand of Satan.

Over the past three years, I have counseled more than 125 people, mostly children and adolescents. While I am a parish priest in Lafayette, Louisiana, I should point out that only a small percentage of these people live in this city; the cases have come from four states, in the South, West and Midwest.

I should also point out that the Satanic cults discussed in this book generally are those considered to be "non-traditionalist" cults. The difference between this type and the "traditionalist" cults — according to claims made by some members of the traditionalist groups — is that many of the non-traditionalists are involved in the sacrificing of human beings and animals, the drinking of animal blood and the ritualistic and sexual abuse of children, while the traditionalists are not involved in this sort of activity. Whether the distinction between the two groups is this clear-cut is debatable, but it is clear that the traditionalist groups have publicly tried to distance themselves from the heinous deeds that some of the non-traditionalists readily admit to.

In addition to informing and cautioning parents and children about the Satanic underworld, this book is an effort to share my experiences as a counselor with priests and others entering this specialized field of counseling. However, this presentation is a broad overview of the subject; the information is generalized and therefore the book should not be used as a counseling guide.

—FATHER JOSEPH BRENNAN

Contents

In memory of my parents,
JOSEPH FRANCIS and KATHRYN ANN BRENNAN,
who, by their love and example,
introduced me to the Kingdom of Light.

*"Draw your strength from the Lord and His mighty power.
Put on the armor of God so that you may be able to stand
firm against the tactics of the devil. Our battle is not against
human forces, but against...the rulers of (the) world of
darkness...."*

—The Epistle of Paul to the Ephesians, 6:10-12.

The Kingdom Of Darkness

Chapter 1

Introduction To The Satanic Underworld

THE PHONE CALL THAT would change my life came in on a cold October morning in 1986. I was working on routine correspondence at my desk in the rectory of Saint Genevieve Catholic Church in Lafayette, Louisiana. I had been pastor there for five years at the time.

The call was from a law-enforcement officer with the local Sheriff's Department. He was investigating a suspicious infant death and three suspicious suicides that had occurred all within a four-month period. He felt that these deaths might be linked to Satanic cults, and he wanted to see me to discuss the supernatural aspects of the cults.

I readily agreed to meet with him that afternoon to discuss the subject, though I was quick to point out that I had little or no knowledge of the subject. Why he chose me, I'm not real sure, except that I consider myself a friend of the sheriff and others in law-enforcement.

In the course of our meeting, the deputy discussed these troublesome cases and raised some questions that made my blood run cold. Could the infant have been sacrificed to Satan? Were the suicides really suicides, or were these young people possibly murdered by fellow members of a Satanic cult because they broke the code of silence — or threatened to do so? Did any of them commit suicide because their sense of worth had been driven so low by the debasing, dehumanizing rituals of cult membership that they felt their lives were not worth living anymore?

Was suicide the only way out of the cult in the minds of any of these kids? Did any of them kill themselves because they wanted to get out of the cult but were terrified by the threats of what would happen to them and/or their loved ones if they attempted to break free? The questions seemed unreal, almost inconceivable; the answers were even more so.

To say that the deputy's visit was disturbing would be a gross understatement. It was through his visit that I was introduced to what I felt could aptly be described as the Kingdom of Darkness.

I felt called to prayer, drawn into meditation. It took time to ponder the reality of this evil kingdom, to accept its reality, to struggle over the question of whether I should get involved in trying to help some of the young victims. I began an extensive study of the subject of Satanic cults and

---

66When a young member wants to get out of a coven, it is difficult for most and impossible for some. Many are held by the threat of death or injury to themselves and/or their loved ones.99

---

the ritualistic abuse of children. The more I read, the more
I understood the power of the Evil One and the nature and
extensiveness of his kingdom on this earth.

I began to understand how young people are recruited
into the Satanic covens by the lure of power; I learned of
the initiation ceremonies that involve the consumption of
blood and urine. When a young member wants to get out
of a coven, it is difficult for most and impossible for some.
Many are held by the threat of death or injury to themselves and/or their loved ones. Others are blackmailed with
the promise that certain embarrassing or illegal activities
they were involved in will be made public if they dare to
leave.

The more I learned about this subject, the more I
realized there was to learn. The more I learned, the more I
felt for the children who had been ritualistically abused and
the young people who were trapped in the cults. Those
who did manage to get out of the cult would need a special
kind of counseling to restore their sense of self-worth, the
sense that God and their fellowman love them, or that they
are loveable or valuable at all. I became convinced that without a special kind of spiritual-based counseling, it would be
nearly impossible for these young people to lead mentally
and spiritually healthy lives.

In the course of my studies, I read a book co-authored by
Dr. Lawrence Pazder and Michelle Smith, titled "Michelle
Remembers." It is a book about Michelle, the co-author,
who was ritualistically abused at an early age and later became possessed by the devil. She was exorcised by the
Bishop of Victoria, British Columbia. Dr. Pazder is an ex-
pert on the subject of Satanic cults and ritualistic abuse.

Because of his knowledge on these subjects, I went to
British Columbia to study under him on several occasions
since 1986. My return flight from the first visit was a time of
decision. Was I being called by God to become a counselor

❝This book is an attempt to expose this sinister underworld and to educate children and parents to be on guard against the quick, elusive hand of the Evil One.❞

to those whose lives had been severely afflicted by Satan? If I began to counsel these people, would the demand for counseling grow to the point that I would have to give up that which I love most on this earth — my duties as a parish priest? If I decided to stop learning about this whole evil business and to give up the idea of becoming a counselor, would I be rejecting a call from God to help the children victimized by the Evil One and his followers?

The conflict has been resolved. With considerable prayer and reflection, I decided to enter the field of counseling. I now spend time both as a counselor and as a parish priest. I have counseled more than 125 people: many children who are victims of ritualistic abuse; teenagers who got hooked into Satanic cults; some adults who were involved in worshiping Satan of their own free will or who were ritualistically abused at a young age and brainwashed into a life of evil. My caseload is growing every month.

In the process of studying, praying and counseling over the past few years, I have learned much about the Kingdom of Darkness. This book is an attempt to share this knowledge and experience with priests and others who may be considering this type of counseling. It is also an attempt to expose this sinister underworld and to educate children and parents to be on guard against the quick, elusive hand of the Evil One and those whose lives he rules.

22

Chapter 2

Elements And Origin Of The Kingdom Of Darkness

O NE OF THE FIRST
people I saw as a counselor was a young man, age 17, who
was a self-induced Satanist, that is, he deliberately chose to
worship Satan of his own free will. He was not one of those
who was lured into a cult, brainwashed and ritualistically
abused by others. He was, however, introduced to and
drawn into the worship of the devil by another individual.

This fellow had spent three or four years inducing the
presence of Satan through rituals and incantations. After
several years in this type of worship, the presence of Satan
in his life was so predominant that a dual personality was
created in the young man. He could assume his other self,
his evil personality, by willfully inducing a trance. When the
trance set in, his face was lifeless, particularly his eyes, and
there was an air of evil in the face of what seemingly had
been a normal teenager. He terrified and intimidated his
classmates with this trance. He also physically abused smaller children on the school ground; he hit them, pulled their

hair and was generally cruel to them. His parents had to take him out of school.

I had occasion to witness the trance first-hand when his mother brought him to see me. The woman was near despair, as all her efforts to correct this condition in her son had been futile. I spoke with the young man only briefly, and as I did he glared at me with great intensity, then he slipped into the trance. He was in this state about 10 minutes, and during that time I was praying for him. His mother was in the room, too, in my office. All of a sudden, in the next room, a blood-curdling shriek was heard by my secretary. She wasn't just scared by it; she was petrified. The shriek was a terrifying sound, but the fact that no one was there — at least, bodily — made it even more frightening.

Creating sounds like this in other rooms is one of the powers possessed by this self-induced Satanist. He has reportedly displayed various demonic powers to others, though I personally have not witnessed them.

When the young man came out of the trance in my office, he told me he wished to give his life to Lucifer — now and forever. He made it clear that he hadn't come to see me of his own free will. His mother essentially forced him to come, hoping that something could be done to rid him of this Satanic presence. I wasn't able to do much in just one visit, and I haven't seen him since. I spoke with his mother once since then, and she said there had been no change in his condition.

Personally, I feel the young man is dangerous. He is quite capable of doing harm to others, physically, spiritually, psychologically. But he's still walking the streets, and there is no way he can be incarcerated or forced to get help of any kind, since he has passed the sanity tests given to him.

Another case I handled involved a young man who had been involved in a Satanic cult. His father brought him in to see me. He told me the boy constantly talked about Satan and even tried to burn a crucifix in their home.

In talking with the boy in our first meeting, I could see he was gripped with fear. He was terrified. He had been warned by others in the cult that if he told anyone what had happened at the ritual meeting, he would regret it. They promised him that harm would come to him and his family, and to dramatize their serious intent they put a cat in front of him and then gouged out its eyes. He was warned that the same would happen to him if he broke the code of silence. He took the warning to heart.

We met several times, and throughout our sessions I continually assured him of the love that Jesus Christ has for him. Through it all, his fear subsided, his faith grew, and he made great progress at returning to a normal life. He now lives with relatives in another state and is said to be doing well.

Perhaps the most disturbing kind of case I have handled involves the sexual and ritualistic abuse of children — oftentimes by their own parents or other relatives.

One mother, who had heard a television interview I had given on the subject, called me about problems with her nine-year-old daughter. The little girl had spent the summer with her father, and when she returned home she was a different person. The child was having fits that involved sexual exhibitions in front of the mirror. She also seemed to have become obsessed with her own defecation. In school, she was violent and physically abusive to her classmates.

She had nightmares two or three times a week. She dreamed that something evil was chasing her. As the thing was about to get to her, she would wake up screaming and sweating, and would run to her mother's room. The child would then sleep with her mom, and all would be fine until the nightmare returned a night or two later.

After many hours of counseling, she finally revealed the root of the problem. She told me that her father had sexually abused her in a shed behind his house. She said that he was involved in Satanic worship and that he had made her attend the coven gatherings. Not only was she sexually abused at these meetings, but she was forced to participate in debasing rituals that included the drinking of her own urine. She was told that Jesus had been killed and that Lucifer was the ruler now. She was told that she was trash, no good. They tried to brainwash her into thinking that she was evil — and that she was expected to do evil things. This kind of brainwashing is uncovered frequently in cases of ritualistic abuse of children.

I'm happy to report that the child is now on the road to recovery. The counseling, in this case and in similar ones, involves having the victim recall the evil that was done to her and having her understand that it is not she who is evil but the people who did these terrible things to her. It also involves assuring her of her inherent worth and goodness and of God's love for her.

The three cases discussed above are the kind I deal with

on a daily basis in my work as a counselor to those whose lives have been touched by people who live in the Kingdom of Darkness.

This kingdom is more real and more widespread in the United States than is commonly realized. In this country, there are 8,000 covens (small groups of cult members), with membership estimated at more than 100,000 people. And this doesn't count the self-styled, self-induced Satanists who don't belong to the covens.

For the sake of clarity, the people involved in the Kingdom of Darkness can be divided into three distinct categories.

First, there are those who are actively involved members of Satanic cults. This membership, in many cases, means dropping their worship of God and turning to worshiping Satan instead.

Second are the self-induced Satanists. These are people who by their own will have induced the presence of Satan into their lives. They sought out the Evil One and committed themselves to follow and worship him. They don't act as part of a group, though they may have contact with others like themselves.

---

66 The Kingdom of Darkness is more real and more widespread in the United States than is commonly realized. In this country, there are 8,000 covens (small groups of cult members), with membership estimated at more than 100,000 people. 99

Third are the innocent victims of ritualistic abuse. These are people who have had evil inflicted upon them, usually at a young age. Typically, they are sexually abused and their lives are ritualistically handed over to Satan. In many cases the knowledge of this evil burden doesn't surface to the conscious mind until later in life. In some cases it never surfaces, and the victims live their entire lives thinking they are evil — and doing evil things that are consistent with their self-image.

Myths

One of the myths currently held by people interested in Satanic cults is that everybody involved in the Kindom of Darkness is possessed. In fact, cases of possession are very rare. In cases of possession, there is complete control by the Evil One.

In the Kingdom of Darkness, people are captivated and enthralled by Satan and his wiles. There are cases of people being used by Satan, as, for example, those who have had evil thrust upon them through ritualistic abuse. And there are those who are emotionally captivated by the Evil One, such as the self-induced Satanists. In either case, these people always exhibit an anger and aggressiveness. They lack peace and tranquility in their lives. They can portray what seems to be Satanic possession, but for the most part, what looks like possession usually isn't.

Another myth concerns dress and life-style. Those who constantly wear black in public are usually dabblers in the cult — and not genuine members. Same for those who wear Satanic symbol jewelry, such as the inverted cross, the 666 or the pentagram. Hard core members wish to be unknown to others, so their dress and life-style are quite ordinary, so as to avoid attracting attention to themselves.

During the past several years, the music associated with the Satanic is heavy metal music. While this type of music can be used to convey Satanic messages, it would be incorrect to assume that members of these bands or people who seem to enjoy this music are necessarily Satan-worshipers. Some are, however.

Spiritual Origin
of the Kingdom of Darkness

For all of eternity, God has been surrounded by arch-angels. Three of the most often mentioned are Saint Gabriel, the Announcer; Saint Michael, the Defender; and Lucifer, the Light-Bearer.

Gabriel announced the birth of John, the Baptizer, and the birth of the Messiah. He also directed Joseph in a dream to take Mary and the baby Jesus and flee from Bethlehem into Egypt.

Michael is considered to be the patron saint of those who would fight the evil that proceeds from the Kingdom of Darkness. A special prayer asking his help starts with these words: "Saint Michael, the Archangel, defend us in battle. Be our protection against the wickedness and snares of the

31

devil...."

Lucifer is the archangel who fell from God's graces — and subsequently was ousted from the divine presence — because he refused to adore the God-Man, Jesus Christ. Pride was the reason. His expulsion from the Kingdom of Heaven marked the beginning of the Kingdom of Darkness — the supernatural realm ruled by the Evil One.

Some time later, the God-Man was born at Bethlehem in the person of Jesus Christ. Jesus grew to manhood and was carrying out his mission as teacher and redeemer. He was confronted in the Sinai Dessert by Lucifer, who earlier had refused to worship Him. Lucifer tried to bribe Jesus into worshiping him, and Jesus refused. Lucifer also challenged Him to prove that He was God by turning the stones to bread and by throwing Himself from the top of the temple without being harmed. Again Jesus refused to be trapped by the evil designs of Lucifer.

> **66 *Those who constantly wear black in public are usually dabblers in the cult — and not genuine members.* 99**

It is quite clear from the scriptures that Lucifer wished for one thing: He wanted Jesus, the God-Man, to drop His role of Messiah and human being and become a creator — which was contrary to the divine plan of redemption. If Satan had prevailed, the act of redemption would have been void. Jesus, while divine, had to remain totally human to offer His Father the full redemptive act. He had to suffer and die as a human being in order to redeem the human race and enable humankind to attain eternal life.

32

The modern-day followers of Lucifer often do believe in God. But, like their evil leader, they refuse to pay homage to the God-Man, Jesus Christ. They refuse to honor the one who Lucifer refused to honor. They abhor all that Jesus stands for, and they blaspheme His holy name with malice and frequency. Some of them also destroy crucifixes, refuse to have their children baptized, and desecrate the consecrated host during their orgies and other rituals designed to honor Lucifer.

Chapter 3

Satanic Cults: Their Patterns, Paraphernalia And Prey

STORIES OF SATANIC cults meeting in cemeteries at night and participating in orgies may sound like fiction from the pen of Edgar Allen Poe. But, in fact, this kind of activity does occur throughout this country on certain Satanic feast days.

An 18-year-old girl who was involved in this was brought to me for counseling by a friend of hers. The girl, whom I'll call Sue, had been a prostitute in a coven for two years. She said she had had sex with male members of the coven — sometimes several of them in a short span of time — as part of a ritual designed to honor Satan.

When I asked how she got involved with the cult, Sue began by telling me she had been having a lot of trouble and turmoil at home. There was much squabbling and fighting between her and her stepfather. There was no peace in the home, and certainly no love between the two of them. They were constantly at each other's throats. The stress was intense. She felt alienated, unloved, unwanted.

Then along came a young man who professed to care for her. She, in turn, cared for him. She looked upon him as a shelter in a storm. She would do anything for him. She would do anything to keep him.

The young man got involved in a Satanic cult — and Sue followed him in without much resistance. In so doing, she felt she was proving her love for him, cementing their relationship.

The cult represented the family she no longer had. She felt a sense of acceptance and belonging there. They had given her something she really wanted and, in turn, she was asked to give them something they wanted — her body. So she became a prostitute to please other members of the coven.

At the same time, however, Sue was not comfortable in the role of prostitute. She was uneasy about it. She felt that she was betraying herself. Though she didn't let her fellow devil-worshipers know her deepest feelings about this, a long-time friend, whom I'll call Alice, sensed that something was very wrong in Sue's life. Her skin was ashen and colorless, her face was lifeless, she had that far-away look in her eye. She was a deeply troubled young woman — and Alice picked up on that fact.

Alice asked Sue what was wrong, and she said "nothing." A week later, the girl in the cult looked just as bad as before, and again she was asked what was the matter, but the answer was about the same, "Nothing. Just leave me alone and mind your own business." The caring friend persisted, and finally Sue broke down and revealed her secret.

Just about that time, Alice saw me in a television interview. She convinced Sue that she needed to get out of the cult, and that seeing me for counseling would be a step in that direction.

Sue came to me for counseling several times. Like others I have talked with, this girl was afraid to reveal much about the cult — particularly the identity of the other members. In the long process of counseling with her, I assured her that she could leave the past behind, that she didn't have to be a prostitute all her life, that she could be set free from the fear that had enslaved her and the role that had temporarily robbed her of her dignity and self-respect. The counseling proved to be successful. She has left the cult and started a new life. She is alive and well and living in another state.

Not all cases involving Satanic cults that I have seen end up as satisfactorily as this one. Some people who want to get out of the cults never do so because they fear for their lives if they try. Others remain for life because they simply want to worship Satan or because they get pleasure from the people and activities associated with the cult.

The idea of worshiping the devil is certainly a strange and foreign concept to

Pentagram
Perhaps the most widely used Satanic mark, the pentagram symbolizes the morning star, a name taken by Satan. The symbol is said to be used to conjure up evil spirits.

666

Mark
Of The
Beast

The mark of Satan, the beast, the anti-Christ, is made in four ways. In the last book of the Bible, Revelation, Chapter 13, verse 18, the number of the beast is revealed — 666.

most Americans. But as foreign as it may seem, Satanic cults have existed in this country since its very inception. They existed in other countries for hundreds of years before that.

Just as Christian churches have been formed around the world as a means of worshiping Jesus Christ, so too were these other kinds of "churches" founded to worship Satan. These groups are called cults; they are composed of smaller units called covens.

The one thing that all Satanic cults have in common is the worship of the devil. But they vary, sometimes widely, as to purpose, membership and activities. Some low-key covens exist only to invoke and worship Satan, and are not necessarily a direct threat to other people. Others are what could be called expansionists, that is, they actively recruit young people as a means of swelling their own ranks and creating more covens — thus spreading the Kingdom of Darkness. This latter group sometimes contains members who callously and savagely abuse children in rituals designed to honor Satan. This abuse ranges from torture to sexual abuse of children to the sacrificing of newborn infants or other human beings. The cult members who engage in this kind of violence are considered "non-traditional" Satanists, while those who do not are considered "traditional."

Cults also vary in the make-up of their

membership. Some are composed of teenagers and adults; others are for adults only. Some members may be incorrigible, anti-social teenagers, while others are pillar-of-the-community types who may be the president of a bank, a leader in a church, or the otherwise respectable businessperson who's been active in community-betterment projects for many years. You just never know.

While there is not a Satanist behind every tree, Satanic cults do exist throughout America. There are 8,000 covens in this country, or an average of 160 covens per state. Some states have more than their share and others have less.

Each coven ideally has 13 members, so there are more than 100,000 members nationwide, as mentioned in the previous chapter. The impact of some of these covens — the lives they have touched by some of their activities — is just now beginning to be realized, as more and more people are coming forward to reveal what they have seen and been involved in. The psychological, spiritual and physical harm that has resulted from some of the cult activities is staggering. It is practically unbelievable in its gruesomeness and in its extensiveness.

Again, it should be noted that not all covens engage in crimes of violence, but enough of them do to justify keeping a wary eye on all of them.

Knowing who they are is no easy task

Goathead
Symbolizing the horned goat, the goat of Mendes, the scapegoat, this is one of the Satanist's ways of mocking Christ as the lamb who died for the sins of humanity.

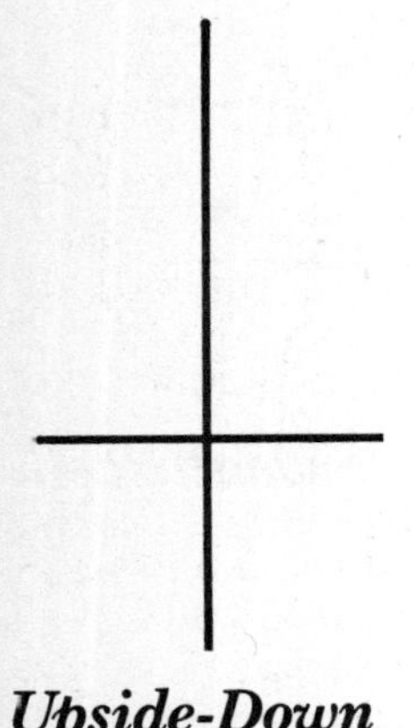

Upside-Down Cross Or Southern Cross

A mockery and rejection of the cross of Christ, this emblem is worn by many Satanists and can be seen on some rock musicians appearing on heavy metal music album covers.

either, because as noted previously, most devoted Satanists are no different in their outward appearance than the average person we see routinely at work or at play. Moreover, the cults are deliberately shrouded in secrecy. They do their thing at night, or behind locked doors, or in remote places where they can't be found out. They often meet in barns and sometimes sacrifice animals there. Their favorite meeting place is in the cemetery, where they celebrate some feast days and carry out their Satanic liturgies.

The secrecy of the cults is protected, in part, by threats of violence to anyone who would inform outsiders about the rites of the cult or the identity of its members. This is quite evident from the reluctance and fear of former cult members to testify.

The ritual leader, or master, can remain unknown even to the membership for his entire tenure. With mask and robe, his identity, profession and place of residence can remain totally unknown to the members.

Although some cult members can and do get caught and prosecuted for acts that are against the law, there is no law that can stop them from worshiping the devil. On the contrary, the First Amendment to the U.S. Constitution, as it is presently interpreted, protects and guarantees them the same freedom of religion as it does all other people in this country. The Constitution doesn't protect only the rights of those engaged in what the majority of Americans consider good and popular forms of worship; it protects the rights of all recognized religions — including the church of Satan.

Recruitment and Initiation

While the age and type of person who may be lured into the occult varies widely, probably the biggest single target group is the impressionable teenager. It's the boy or girl with low self-esteem, usually with vague or confused religious and moral values. It's the young person with lots of idle time on his hands, one not involved in extracurricular activities at school. These people are much easier prey than the young person who is actively involved in his school and church.

Satanists look for people on the fringe areas. These are the ones who are most vulnerable, most impressionable, most readily available to try something new and daring.

They are often approached with this proposition:

"You're not doing anything important. We can show you something that other people don't have."

It is with this type of lure that these young people are brought into their initial meeting of the Satanic cult. They are attracted by the prospect of power, by the promise of belonging.

Scarab Beetle
This is the dung beetle, which is the ancient Egyptian symbol of reincarnation. It is also symbolic of Beelzebub (Satan), Lord of the Flies. It is worn in the occult to show that its holder has power, and it is said to be a source of protection from others within the occultic realm.

43

**Broken
Cross
Or
Peace
Sign**

*This sign represented peace
in the 1960s, but now
among occult groups it
represents the hoped-for
defeat of Christianity —
another way of mocking
Christ.*

From the beginning of their membership, fear tactics are used on them. They are told that if they say anything about where they were and especially about what they were doing, their parents will be harmed or killed — and that the same fate will be theirs.

The initiation ceremony usually involves participation in some type of sexual aberration. They are required to drink their own urine and eat their own defecation. At certain meetings they are required to consume the blood and the sexual organs of animals. They are told that once they do, they will become full-rited members.

The act of consumption of urine, feces and animal blood is so debasing that, in many cases, these young people can never seem to overcome it.

The use of drugs and narcotics with people in the cult usually happens after this initiation ceremony. The dehumanizing effect of the initiation ceremony is eased somewhat by using drugs.

The people who make it through the initiation ceremony are then committed to the worship of the Evil One. They are committed to dropping any allegiance not to God, the Father — because Satanists do believe in God — but to Jesus Christ, whom they are taught to despise.

Behavioral Patterns

When young people are brought into the Satanic cult, the fear and threats that are imposed upon them often overtake their personality. They become withdrawn and, in some cases, aggressive when asked about their whereabouts or about their activities.

The fear and threats used on these people make them almost impossible to counsel. They become strangely mute and almost distant when spoken to.

One of the signs of cult involvement is the constant need to draw and sketch the symbols of the Satanic cult. Another of the signs is an obsession with walking through graveyards — because it is there that they participated in some of the cult's rituals.

But above all, the most common sign is the demand that their room be locked and no one allowed to enter. This is often the telltale sign of either self-induced Satanism or actual membership in Satanic cults. I have never seen a case where they have not had this demand for secrecy concerning their room. The tragedy is when something happens to these young people, and only later is the room opened and the Satanic paraphernalia discovered.

It is of paramount importance for parents who suspect an entanglement of their

**Satanic Cross,
Or Cross
Of Confusion**
An ancient Roman symbol questioning the validity of Christianity and/or the deity of God.

*Satanic S
Or
Broken S*

This represents a thunderbolt and means "destroyer." It was worn by the members of the feared death squads of Nazi Germany.

children with the Satanic cult to make sure that all rooms in their homes are open.

One day in 1988 I was called to a treatment center to see a 16-year-old girl suspected of being a member of a Satanic cult. Her parents had her committed to the center because of her aggressive and seemingly unreasonable behavior toward them. She insisted on keeping her bedroom door locked and demanded that no one else be allowed in. She asserted that she had a right to privacy and gave them that you-don't-trust-me routine designed to manipulate them and make them feel guilty.

The parents were having a harder and harder time trusting her as her behavior became increasingly suspicious — and aggressive — where this privacy issue was concerned.

Once the girl was in the treatment center and beginning counseling, the parents broke into the room. They found it filled with the paraphernalia of Satanic worship — a drawing of the goat's head, black candles, the pentagram and all the rest.

The girl continues to see a counselor, and hopefully she will be brought back to a life of joy and normality.

Satanic Paraphernalia

People in Satanic cults use a wide array of paraphernalia in connection with their recognition and worship of the Evil One. These include black robes, black candles, books on the occult, jewelry with Satanic symbols and posters bearing all kinds of Satanic symbols and messages.

Black candles, which signify death, and red candles, which signify lust, are used in various Satanic ceremonies. So are black robes. Hard core Satanists confine their use of these candles and clothing to their Satanic rites. Since they make considerable efforts to hide their identity as members of the cult, they wouldn't use these items in public. The same is true of jewelry bearing Satanic symbols, such as the pentagram, the 666, the inverted cross and the like.

Posters bearing these same Satanic symbols or Satanic themes, as well as books about the occult, are used by cult members, though possession of these items doesn't necessarily prove cult membership.

During the past several years, heavy metal music has been closely identified with the occult. The music can be dangerous, in that it can be a significant factor leading to interest in sadism and violence and actual involvement in evil deeds. Some heavy metal musicians have publicly identified themselves as Satanists, and some of their lyrics reflect themes of destruction and violence. Of course, the fact that young people play the music and have the albums doesn't necessarily mean they are members of a cult.

**Swastika,
Or
Sun Wheel**
The emblem of Nazi Germany, led by Adolph Hitler — one of the world's most infamous Satanists. Long before Hitler came to power, however, it was an ancient religious symbol used in Buddhist inscriptions, Celtic monuments and Greek coins. In sun god worship, it is supposed to represent the sun's course in the heavens.

Satanic Ritual Calendar

DATE	CELEBRATION	TYPE	AGE/GENDER/SPECIES
Jan. 7	St. Winebald Day	Blood	15-33 (male, if human)
Jan. 17	Satanic Revels	Sexual	7-17 (female)
Feb. 2	Satanic Revels	Sexual	7-17 (female)
Feb. 25	St. Walpurgis Day	Blood	Animal
March 1	St. Eichatadt	Blood	Any age (male or female)
March 20	Feast Day (Spring Equinox)	Orgies	Any age (male or female, human or animal)
April 21-26	Preparation for the sacrifice		
April 26-May 1	Grand Climax	Da Meur	1-25 (female)
June 21	Feast Day (Summer Solstice)	Orgies	Any age (male or female, human or animal)
July 1	Demon Revels	Blood	Any age (female)
Aug. 3	Satanic Revels	Sexual	7-17 (female)
Sept. 7	Marriage to the Beast, Satan	Sexual	Infant to 21 (female)
Sept. 20	Midnight Host	Blood	Infant to 21 (female)
Sept. 22	Feast Day (Fall Equinox)	Orgies	Any age (male or female, human or animal)
Oct. 29-Nov. 1	All Hallow Eve (Halloween)	Blood Sexual	Any age (male or female)
Nov. 4	Satanic Revels	Sexual	7-17 (female)
Dec. 22	Feast Day	Orgies	Any age (male or female, human or animal)
Dec. 24	Demon Revels	Da Meur	Any age (male or female)

Source: Passport Magazine, 1432 W. Puente Ave., West Covina, Calif. 91790

Many of those who play the music, wear the clothing and jewelry in public, hang the posters and buy the books are only dabbling. We have a society of dabblers. Young people go through different stages in their lives, and many of them dabble in this and in that. But dabbling in the occult can be dangerous. Dabblers run the risk of going further and becoming more involved in the Kingdom of Darkness.

When young people are found dabbling, they should be counseled. They should be made aware of the dangers involved — by parents, by pastors or by their school counselors. They should be made aware of what can happen to people who experience the reality of the initiation ceremonies in the Satanic cult.

Feast Days, Rituals and Symbols

Most covens have feast days that are close to the calendar of the Catholic Church. The activities performed on these days depend on the nature of the feast. On certain feast days animals are used, and on other days sexual orgies are engaged in. It is difficult to cite the particular ceremony that would take place in a certain coven, because this varies.

Almost every coven has some type of ritual ceremony on All Saints Day and All Souls Day. The Feast of the Beast doesn't come every year but is of major importance in their ritual and their worship.

Udjat,
Or All-Seeing
Eye
A symbol that refers to Lucifer, the king of hell. The eye is half closed, illustrating that even though you may not think the devil is watching you, he is. Below the eye is a tear, because he "mourns" for those outside of his influence.

Perhaps the most disturbing ritual known to be performed by the coven is the Black Mass. In this ceremony the Holy Eucharist is placed on the nude body of one of the female members during an orgy. There is evidence that cult members steal the consecrated hosts, especially during Sunday liturgies, and take these hosts to their meetings for desecration.

Each coven adopts their own special Satanic symbols, but the sign of the pentagram, the 666 and the upside down cross are universal in their usage.

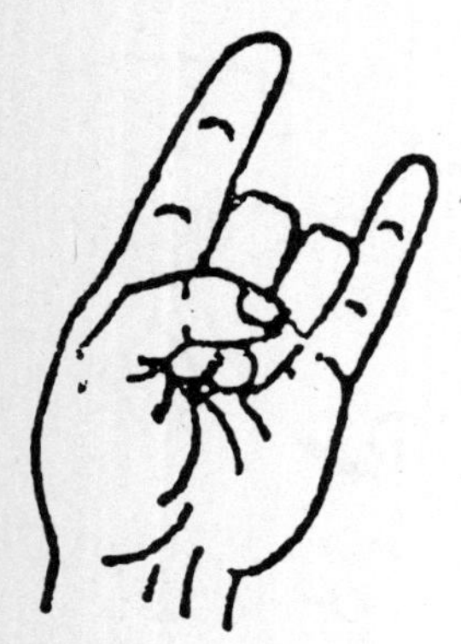

Horned Hand

This is a sign of recognition among those who are in the occult. It may also be innocently used by those who identify with heavy metal music, as well as fans of the Texas Longhorns athletic teams.

Chapter 4

The Self-Induced Satanist

IN ALL MY DEALINGS WITH people who live in the Kingdom of Darkness, none was more frightening than the time I attempted to counsel a self-styled Satanist who was brought to me in chains and shackles.

The man, age 29, had been arrested and was in jail on multiple charges of rape and assault. He was accused of beating women into submission and then raping them — on eight different occasions. He said he did it to please Satan and to gain souls for him.

The social worker assigned to the case was scared to death of the man. The police, too, were very wary of this person. He was constantly drawing Satanic symbols on the walls of his cell. He also had a habit of drinking his own urine and eating his own defecation — a ritual designed to honor the Prince of Darkness. He claimed that Satan visited him every night. He told the police he wished to die so that he might be Satan's servant forever.

Knowing this about the man, I felt that the meeting with

him might be difficult — to put it mildly — so I prepared myself for it through much prayer and meditation. The night before the meeting, I also phoned the person who trained me in this work so that I would be assured of my approach.

The next morning, the police brought the man into my office, and they waited outside at my request. There were three officers, and the one in charge seemed reluctant to leave me alone with the man, but I said that's the way it would have to be. They waited just outside my door.

This worshiper of the devil was a small man, maybe 120 pounds, if that. He was dark-haired and unshaven, and his eyes were extremely dark, nearly black. There was an air of evil about him as he entered the room. He had a far-away look in his eyes, like he wasn't really present, almost as if he were possessed. I'll never forget that look. I'll never forget the way he stared at me with those evil eyes.

Yet, I felt nothing but pity for this poor soul. Here was a human being so captivated by Satan that he had taken on the appearance of evil itself. He looked like evil personified. It would take a lot of doing to keep this man's soul from the fires of hell.

I spoke with him for about 20 minutes. I tried to get him to talk with me, but he didn't say much. As it turned out, I did most of the talking. I spoke to him with concern and compassion, as a priest would speak with someone who was incarcerated. I noticed a tear coming down his face. I felt like I was getting somewhere, making some progress. Then I told him that Jesus loves him.

Upon hearing the word "Jesus," the man went wild. Even though he was chained, he lunged at me like a vicious animal, spitting and grunting and clawing his way over my desk. I shoved him back and shouted for help. The police rushed in and one of them grabbed him. He kept coming at me and spitting at me. The other two grabbed him, but even the three of them couldn't restrain this little man of 120 pounds. They called for a back-up, and a fourth officer came in. Together, they were able to wrestle him to the ground, still kicking and spitting and grunting like a hog.

Once he was down and seemingly under control, he continued spitting, so they wrapped a towel around his face and head then forced him out of the building and into the police van.

In my limited dealings with this man, I wasn't able to find out much about his background. So, I don't know exactly what it was that led him to worship Satan. But I do know that he is a self-induced Satanist — and that I shall never, never forget that evil stare.

I wish I could have helped him find his way out of the darkness in which he dwelled.

Self-induced, or self-styled, Satanists are different from those in a cult in that they are not part of an organized group. They can be exactly like cult worshipers except for the fact they they act alone.

Why alone? Sometimes it is because they tried to get into a cult but were rejected because those in the cult didn't like them or didn't trust that they could keep the code of secrecy. Sometimes it is because they didn't trust the cult members or they simply preferred to act on their own. Sometimes it is because there were no cults operating in their locale, or if there were, they simply didn't know it.

Some of these people come to be self-induced Satanists with the aid and guidance of other self-induced Satanists. Others learn how by studying books on the occult.

Though they aren't in a cult, their behavior closely resembles the behavior of those who are. They are often obsessed with the consumption of urine and defecation, as well as with the drawing of Satanic symbols.

Just as Christians seek to draw closer to Christ by prayer, good works and the spirit of sacrifice, so too do Satanists attempt to draw closer to Satan through incantations and various rituals. In some cases, Satanists have the power to tell other people all about their past — though there is no way they could have known through natural means.

56

Like the members of Satanic cults, these people who are drawn into the worship of the devil typically have low self-esteem, and/or were reared in an amoral fashion and/or were not active participants in their church.

Others may have suffered from some type of emotional or physical trauma, such as being rejected by a girlfriend, losing a parent at a young age or being crippled or maimed for life in a car accident. They feel that God has turned His back on them by allowing this terrible thing to happen to them, so they turn their back on God — with a vengeance.

Some people who are self-styled, individual Satanists are survivors of sexual and ritualistic abuse who, through no fault of their own, had an evil burden placed on them by members of a cult. This burden, this feeling that they are evil, often resurfaces later in life, and they feel driven to find a means of expressing the evil within. Accordingly, they seek out the Evil One and act out the evil deeds that are consistent with their self-image.

Some people worship Satan because they believe he will give them powers that others don't have. Others do it as a means of rebelling against Christian parents or other authority figures. Still others have a psychotic desire to be religiously different.

Some simply fall into it. They get pulled into the worship of Satan while dabbling in the occult.

Chapter 5

The Innocent Victims Of Ritualistic Abuse

R ITUALISTIC ABUSE
of children is perhaps the most disturbing aspect of the underworld we know as the Kingdom of Darkness.

It's one thing when a person, of his own free will, chooses
to dedicate his life to the worship of Satan and turns to a
life of evil. It's quite another when this person attempts to
gain souls for Satan by ritualistically abusing innocent children — brainwashing them into believing they are bad and
programming them for a life of evil thoughts and evil
deeds. This has got to be one of the most grievous, most
immoral offenses a human being can commit.

Jesus was crystal clear about how He viewed people who
do things to harm innocent children: "It would be better
for anyone who leads astray one of these little ones who believe in me, to be drowned by a millstone around his neck,
in the depths of the sea.... Woe to that man through whom
scandal comes!" (Matthew 18:6,7)

I have counseled dozens of victims of ritualistic abuse,

both children and adults who were abused as children. To me, there is nothing sadder in the world than to hear the stories that these people tell. There is nothing more distressing than to see a child who — as a result of ritualistic and/or sexual abuse — has been robbed of the joy of childhood.

It is no accident, no incidental by-product of Satanic rites, that children are deprived of their natural joy, exuberance and optimism. Non-traditional Satanists do it deliberately; they replace these bright qualities with fear, sadness, pessimism and self-loathing. This is done to program the children, to prepare them for a life in Satanic covens. It is a means of implanting an evil self-concept in their subconscious minds to assure that they will do evil and not good in the years ahead, even if they don't end up in a Satanic cult.

As appalling and horrendous as it is, ritualistic abuse is not a rare phenomenon. It is commonly practiced by many non-traditional Satanic cults throughout the United States and elsewhere. It is a means of attempting to gain souls for Satan.

Ritualistic abuse involves forcing a child to do something against his will, usually something repulsive or offensive to the normal sensibilities of decent people. For example, forcing him to eat his own feces or drink his own urine, eat an animal's sexual organs or even consume the flesh of a human corpse.

Closely allied to ritual abuse is sexual abuse of the children. Practically any kind of sexual abuse imaginable has been done to children somewhere in this country.

One of the many cases of ritualistic abuse I handled came to me from a neighboring state in the summer of 1988. The child had been the victim of horrible sexual abuse and ritualistic torture. The sexual abuse was so brutal, in fact, that it required surgery to repair the anus that tore as a result of the torture.

“*Ritualistic abuse involves forcing a child to do something against his will, usually something repulsive or offensive to the normal sensibilities of decent people.*”

If that were not enough to psychologically scar him for the rest of his life, the child was also forced to witness the birth and death of a newborn baby; the infant was murdered, sacrificed as an offering to Satan. He was also made to drink the blood of animals on many occasions, as part of the coven's ritual.

It is going to take many months, even years, to handle this case because of the severity of the harm that was done to this boy when he was a child. Though this happened to him several years before, he still has spells of extreme fear and anxiety, and his mouth breaks out in ulcers — usually on Satanic feast days.

In another case, a mother and stepfather brought a young boy to me because they were concerned about what they considered "very abnormal behavior." He was showing an obsession with his own defecation, followed by fits of aggressiveness and violence toward others. One of the cruelest things he was doing was tripping his elderly grandmother in hopes that she would fall and hurt herself. He was caught doing this several times, yet he denied it. He lied constantly about this, about his whereabouts and about other matters as well.

He was truthful in the counseling sessions, however. We discussed his present life and feelings, then we went back through the years, working back a year at a time, to the time when he was with his natural father. At this stage, the child became nearly rigid. I gave him assurances that it was okay to talk about what was disturbing him. Once he became somewhat comfortable with that idea, he poured out the story that I had suspected was the cause of his abnormal behavior. He told me that he had been physically and ritualistically abused by his father, in a barn. His father, who was either a member of a Satanic cult or else a self-induced Satanist, had attempted to hand the boy over to the devil in a series of rituals. He remembered seeing the black candles and the ever-present pentagram. He told me that the rituals involved drinking of his own urine and the consumption of the blood of an animal, probably a dog.

Throughout our sessions, the boy was reminded of the love that Jesus Christ has for him. He listened closely as I pointed out that the evil burden he was carrying was not something he chose but rather something that was forced upon him. It took him a while to accept this idea but he finally did accept it — and he quit blaming himself for the things that happened in that barn. He has responded well to counseling and is healing more and more each month.

The Evil Burden

The purpose of ritualistic abuse is to win souls for Satan and to perpetuate Satanic cults. With the continual bombardment of physical and psychological abuse, the Satanist tries to impose an evil burden upon the mind of the victim — almost as though a spell were being cast upon him, though it is more like brainwashing.

A Satanist inflicts his victim with an evil burden by forcing him to do debasing and dehumanizing things and thus brainwashing him into thinking that he is no good, that he himself is evil, and that he is naturally expected to act in evil ways. When we speak of the evil burden we are speaking of this warped self-concept, this terrible self-image, that is forced upon innocent people, particularly children, with the use of various Satanic rituals.

It is more than just a negative self-concept, though. This evil burden is so powerful, it becomes so pronounced, that it takes on a life of its own. It becomes something akin to a second personality. It is a force that can completely take over a child's personality — and it frequently does.

It is almost as if the evil burden becomes personified, allowing the spirit and the will of Satan to be expressed through the thoughts and actions of the victim.

The manner in which this evil burden affects the victim's personality is so pronounced that therapists have sometimes mistakenly diagnosed their patients as being manic-depressive, schizophrenic or having multiple personalities.

Other therapists, not experienced in counseling ritualistically abused children, have failed to understand the phenomenon of the evil burden and have concluded erroneously that their patients were possessed by the devil. In one case, an exorcist was called in to try to cast out the

---

" *The child's condition improved greatly when the proper remedy was applied — when he was counseled, the evil burden was exposed, memories of the abusive episodes were dealt with, and he was assured of his own inherent goodness and value and of the love that God has for him.* "

---

devil. The exorcism was performed — but nothing happened. The therapist concluded that Satan had won out and that evil had prevailed. The fact is that exorcism was ineffective because the child was not possessed by the devil, but rather was afflicted by the evil burden that resulted from ritualistic abuse.

Later, the child's condition improved greatly when the proper remedy was applied — when he was counseled, the evil burden was exposed, memories of the abusive episodes were dealt with and he was assured of his own inherent goodness and value and of the love that God has for him.

In the cases I have counseled, I have found a tendency on the part of the victims to suppress the evil burden, to push it out of their conscious mind, because it is so difficult and painful to deal with. While many succeed in pushing it from their conscious mind, it remains lodged in their subconscious mind — and it still affects the manner in which they think and act, to one degree or another.

This evil burden may remain suppressed for one, two, five, ten or 30 years, depending on a variety of factors. It usually emerges from the subconscious at a time of physical or emotional tragedy, like the loss of a loved one, a miscarriage or some other emotional upheaval. It can also be drawn out through counseling. It is then that the person becomes consciously aware of something inside his or her mind that is unusual, unsettling or disturbing.

Their behavior may be hostile, aggressive and unpleasant while the burden is buried in the unconscious mind, but it can become even more so once this burden begins to emerge and floods the conscious mind with memories of the evil that was done to them and thoughts of the evil that they might do to others. At this point, they are thinking of themselves as evil, and their minds are conjuring up thoughts of evil deeds.

As the evil thoughts and the evil self-image emerge and

try to take over the personality, they come in conflict with the thoughts and self-image of a person who perceives himself as being good. Thus, there is a battle between good and evil going on in the mind and heart of the person. It is a spiritual battle between a life filled with the grace of God and a life dominated by the influences of the Evil One. This conflict is cause for irritability, for confusion, for aggressiveness.

The Signs of Ritualistic Abuse

Abnormal behavior can be seen in ritualistically abused people during, before or after the time that the evil burden is dislodged from their subconscious mind. In my time as a counselor, I have observed four distinct signs that point to the potential existence of the evil burden.

1. Obsession with urine and defecation. It is common for victims of abuse to wrap their own feces in a towel or sheet or to otherwise hide it away to be touched and handled later. Why they do this is not easy to understand, but it should be noted that it was in the area of the groin that many of these people were harmed during Satanic rituals.

2. Abnormal fits of exhibitionism. This includes running around the house naked and/or nude performances in front of a mirror, such as dancing and lewd gestures. This is one of the kinds of things they were pushed into doing during the rituals.

3. Long periods of rage and over-aggressiveness. This aggressiveness can be caused by the simple presence of the evil burden — or by its emergence from the subconscious mind. The target of these people's rage may be parents, siblings, neighbors, classmates or others. They would naturally like to attack the ones who put this burden on them, but they can't because the perpetrators are nowhere to be found. The abuse may have happened one, two, five, ten or even 30 years before. So they attack whoever happens to be around. This is what is known as misplaced aggression or misdirected aggression.

They feel they can't get relief from this burden by talking about it, either. For one thing, they may feel ashamed, as if they had done something wrong and dirty by their own choice. For another thing, they fear that to tell what happened to them when they were forbidden to tell might bring on more harm or even death to themselves or those they care about.

They feel trapped, frustrated. On a conscious level, they feel they cannot ask for help, but on a subconscious level — where the drive for life and self-preservation is always at work — they do cry out for help by acting in an over-aggressive manner. Simply put, this behavior is a cry for help. This is their way of asking for help. It is a subconscious effort at spritual and psychological self-preservation.

4. Negative attitude toward morality stemming from an evil that is sensed internally. Because the victim of ritual abuse has been brainwashed into thinking he is bad, evil, dirty, he literally believes himself to be that way. As a result, he perceives good and moral thoughts and behavior as inconsistent with his own self-image. Convinced that he himself is evil, he has a negative attitude toward what is good — and he acts out this belief in various forms of immoral, cruel and/or anti-social behavior.

The Iceberg Theory

I have counseled many victims of ritualistic abuse from several parts of the United States, and I have come to the conclusion that no part of the country has been spared from this blight. The problem is widespread.

The voices of those who have been abused are just now starting to be heard. For every voice we have heard, I believe there are 10, 20, 30 or more that are silent.

Each case is only a variation on a common theme that involves the immoral and illegal abuse of children. To understand what I mean, consider these cases from the files of people I have counseled:

• A 10-year-old boy was used in an X-rated film, he witnessed the sacrifice of a newborn baby, was sexually abused, was urinated on in a ritual and forced to drink the blood of an animal. While being counseled, he had a spell and fell on the floor. His mouth broke out in ulcers. He was given a crucifix and he tried to set it on fire.

• A small girl was sexually abused in a Satanic ritual by an employee of a daycare center. She was made to view adults engaged in sexual activities and told to do the same with another child — though she was maybe five-years-old at the time. She was told that she was going to die soon; now she draws pictures of a grave with her name on the headstone. She's hyperactive and difficult to deal with in school and, not surprisingly, doesn't trust adults.

• A 15-year-old-boy has abnormal toilet habits and violent rages and shows signs of sexual exhibitionism after talking about the abuse done to him by an adult. He displays multiple personalities; signs of real and imagined people come out in him 15 to 30 minutes after he goes into a trance. One of these personalities is that of a deceased uncle, who urges him to harm other people.

• A brother and sister were sexually and ritualistically abused by an uncle who was considered to be a prominent member of a Midwestern community. The man, a member of a Satanic cult, violated these children at the tender ages of 5 and 7. Both children showed signs of sexual exhibitionism and violent temper tantrums — especially on Satanic feast days — with uncontrollable, nearly psychotic, screaming, ranting and raving.

• A 40-year-old man — a survivor of ritualistic abuse — came to see me for counseling after carrying that burden for 30 years. He was brought into a Satanic coven at a young age, held for eight days and ritualistically abused by being forced to drink animal blood and participate in sexual aberrations and other parts of the ritual.

• A little girl was victimized by a babysitting service employee who wore a black robe during Satanic rituals. She was told that the devil had killed Jesus and that only stupid people wear crosses. The child was made to undress and perform lewd dances in front of a mirror. She was brought to counseling because she was playing with her own feces and exhibiting other abnormal toilet habits.

The presence and extensiveness of ritualistic and sexual abuse is an ugly scar upon the face of our nation. It is being reported more and more with each passing year. It is something that has been with us for many, many years.

It was kept relatively quiet because the children were afraid to talk. They had no one to tell; almost no one wanted to hear it. Hardly anyone knew how to handle these complaints even when they were brought forth.

❝I believe we are just now beginning to see the tip of the iceberg in terms of the number of children who have been abused. For every voice we have heard, I believe there are 10, 20, 30 or more that are silent. I predict there will be an explosion of cases reported in the 1990s. I look for an increase in the number of support groups for survivors of sexual and ritualistic abuse all over America.❞

I believe we are just now beginning to see the tip of the iceberg in terms of the number of children who have been abused. More children are coming forward with their stories — and they're being heard and believed by adults. When victims of ritualistic abuse hear and see other victims stepping forward and telling their stories, they themselves are encouraged to speak up and to seek help to heal the deep psychological wounds which they have borne in silence for so many years.

I predict there will be an explosion of cases reported in the 1990s. From what I have seen in only three years, I think the number of cases reported will be staggering — and sickening to people of normal sensibilities. As a result, I look for an increase in the number of support groups for survivors of sexual and ritualistic abuse all over America. I predict there will be many more counselors entering this specialized field.

I predict — and I pray — that many of those responsible for these crimes against innocent children will be brought to justice. I hope that ways will be found to reform and rehabilitate these lost souls. I hope that we can eradicate any and all abuse of children, though I am not optimistic that it will happen in my lifetime.

Chapter 6

Advice For Parents

*I*N MY YEARS OF INVOLVE-
ment with those harmed by the Kingdom of Darkness, I have spoken to many groups. A large portion of these groups were parents who were concerned with whether their children were involved in Satanic worship or related activities. Other parents wanted to know how to prevent this danger from touching the lives of their children.

It isn't always easy to determine if your children are involved in Satanic worship, but some of the things to look out for, which were discussed in detail in Chapter 3, include these:

• Strong demands that their rooms be locked and no one allowed to enter.

• Aggressiveness when asked about their whereabouts and activities.

• Sudden and complete disinterest in going to church.

• Constant need to sketch Satanic symbols.

• Satanic jewelry such as the inverted cross, the 666, the

pentagram.
- Books on the occult.
- Black candles.
- Black robes.
- Posters with Satanic symbols and messages.
- Obsession with walking through graveyards.

As mentioned in a previous chapter, many young people who buy books on the occult, wear jewelry with Satanic symbols in public or constantly listen to heavy metal music are only dabbling. But dabbling in the occult can be extremely dangerous; it can lead to actual and active involvement in a Satanic cult.

If you find your children dabbling or if you have reason to believe they're doing more than just dabbling, by all means contact your pastor or a counselor and discuss a plan of action to prevent further involvement.

The surest way to avoid the Kingdom of Darkness from entering your home is to have your home as a place of prayer and a center of communications. When family prayer is practiced and when communication abounds, there is little or no danger that the Evil One will come through the portals of your home.

On the subject of communication, always be aware that there is a difference between listening to your children and just hearing them. There is a big difference between saying, "It's okay to do your own thing," and giving them the time

---

❝The surest way to avoid the Kingdom of Darkness from entering your home is to have your home as a place of prayer and a center of communications.❞

---

to sit down and share with you as their parents. This is how to keep the lines of communication open; this is a real act of love and a sincere gesture of interest in and concern for your child's well-being. This is especially important when you consider that one of the favorite targets of cult recruiters is unhappy children — young people who feel unloved and/or alienated from their parents, their families, their homes.

Let your house be a house of prayer — and let your Sundays be a time of the family worshiping at church together. Inevitably, your children are going to disappoint you at times as they grow into maturity, but never let them feel that you have abandoned your commitment to prayer, to communication and to their overall well-being.

Young people who are lured into Satanic cults are often those who are not involved in their church or any extracurricular activities at school. It's true, as the old saying goes, "The idle mind is the devil's workshop." So, encourage them to get involved in choir, band, debate, 4-H, athletics or whatever. This will help keep them from loitering on the streets or in the pool halls, video arcades and shopping malls — all of which are the hunting grounds for those who recruit young people into their cults.

As mentioned earlier in this book, I feel that ritualistic abuse of children is perhaps the most disturbing aspect of the Kingdom of Darkness. While it may be difficult to determine if your child is involved in a cult, it can be doubly difficult to ascertain for sure whether he or she has been ritualistically and/or sexually abused. The signs to look for, as explained in detail in Chapter 5, are:
 • Obsession with urine and defecation
 • Abnormal fits of exhibitionism
 • Long periods of rage and over-aggressiveness
 • Negative attitude toward morality stemming from an evil that is sensed internally.

If any of these signs are evident in your child's behavior, a pastor or counselor should be contacted promptly.

In some areas of the country there are support groups for survivors of ritualistic abuse. There is a group called Incest Survivors Anonymous. Another one, which is spreading throughout the country is called Believe the Children; its purpose is to listen to — and act on — the reports of children who speak of being ritualistically and/or sexually abused. (See appendix for addresses and phone numbers.)

I have been asked on several occasions about the possible danger of the board game, Dungeons & Dragons, Ouija boards and the reading of books on Satanism. I feel that they are dangerous, and my advice is to stay away from them all.

In my opinion, and in the opinion of others, Dungeons & Dragons and other fantasy role-playing games can lead to serious involvement in the Kingdom of Darkness — and eventually to crime. Dozens of deaths in this country have been linked to the playing of Dungeons & Dragons, according to Dr. Thomas E. Radecki, an Illinois psychiatrist and research director for the National Coalition on Television Violence. It begins as a board game, but it can lead to acting out the game in real life; it can be dangerous when the "dungeon master" has evil intent or criminal designs.

If your children do happen to stray into the Kingdom of Darkness, don't lose hope. I believe strongly that love can

bring them back — your love and the love of God. The one
thing that those in the Kingdom of Darkness wish to take
from your children is the ability to love and to be loved. I
have never seen a child brought to me for counseling who
does not have this urge to love again and to be loved again.
Supply that love in your home and in their lives, and you
can be confident that, with the help of God's grace, they can
be brought back from the darkness.

Chapter 7

A Word To Counselors

IN COUNSELING PEOPLE WHO live or have lived in the Kingdom of Darkness, it is very important to appreciate the fact that you are dealing with people who were hurt — and hurt deeply.

This pain was either brought on by themselves, of their own free will, such as in cases of self-styled Satanists, or else it was forced upon them against their will, such as in cases of ritualistic abuse. In either case, the counseling approach should be gentle, positive and prayerful.

To experience any degree of success in these kinds of cases, I have found that a real trust must be established. Offering quiet assurances to the person that he or she is going to be healed by a loving God is central to establishing this trust. Another important element is time: This healing process cannot be rushed if it is going to be successful. The hurt that will be revealed will come out slowly. Waiting five minutes or more for a response to your questions is more the rule than the exception. So, any over-anxiousness on the part of the counselor to get to the bottom of the case will almost surely prove to be counterproductive.

In cases of ritualistic abuse, the fact of the matter is that evil was thrust upon the victim against his will, as opposed to his doing evil of his own accord. This should be explained to the victim as many times as necessary. A realization of this basic concept is essential to the victim's complete emergence from the pain and darkness in which he lived. Be aware, too, that to urge the person to confess or to express sorrow for his actions would be to place guilt where it doesn't belong.

I have found in counseling these cases that the more we went into the harmful events of the past, the more evident it became that the person was weighted down by an evil burden and saddled with an evil self-concept. The clearer this became to me, the more I felt called to prayer and the more fervent my prayer became. (See Chapter 5 for a definition and discussion of the evil burden.)

I have also found that as we rooted out this evil burden, identified it and brought it forth for examination, that it started to lose its grip on the mind and the soul of its victim. Its power began to melt away as it was held up to the warm, bright light of God's love and grace. Each time this happened, I was reminded all over again that the benevolent, loving God who created us stands waiting with open arms to welcome us all to the Kingdom of Light — and that this invitation is also open to people who dwell or have dwelled in the Kingdom of Darkness, whether by their own choice or against their will.

In many cases, the evil self-concept that burdens the victim has been mistaken for schizophrenia or multiple personality disorders by physicians and therapists not experienced in this kind of counseling. But, in fact, it is the conflict between the presence of evil and the life of grace that is causing this seemingly schizophrenic experience.

When treating these cases, it is of the utmost importance to never directly encounter nor confront the Evil One. It is vitally important that Satan not be addressed, not be recognized, not be answered. To encounter him, to acknowledge his presence, gives him a power that should not be his.

Instead of confronting the Evil One, the affirmative approach should be taken: The presence of God in this person should be invoked and focused upon. The grace of God that lives within this person should be emphasized. Assurances should be given that this person is indeed still loved by God — and loved very dearly.

As a Catholic priest, my approach has included not only the general affirmation of God's love for the person, but also the use of the sacraments, as a means of bringing the person to the realization of God's presence in his life. I have employed the Sacrament of Reconciliation, where appropriate, and the Sacrament of the Sick in many cases. In all cases I have tried to make them aware that the love of Jesus Christ is theirs and that He will free them from their fear and bondage if they will only ask.

When possible cases of ritualistic abuse are presented to the counselors, one way to diagnose the case is to obtain answers to some vital questions: Do they wish to let go of the past? Do they long for peace of mind? Do they wish to cast off the fear that plagues them?

As the counseling goes on, it is important that the approach remain gentle and soft-spoken. If these people are confronted harshly in a battle with Satan, they are going to regress — and the chances for helping them will be greatly reduced. The pastoral approach, the promise that Jesus can take away their fears, has been effective for me in my ministry as a counselor.

> **❝If these people are confronted harshly in a battle with Satan, they are going to regress.❞**

In cases of ritualistic abuse, the counselor may encounter some hesitancy on the part of the victim to let go of the evil burden present within. If this burden has been in this person for a number of years, he may fear that its removal will upset his life or will bring on some type of retaliation from the people who helped put it there. However, this resistance to letting go of the evil burden can be overcome by assuring him of the love that God has for him; it can be overcome by convincing him that, if he will ask for it, a feeling of joy and a sense of being good and valuable will take the place of the feelings of evil and worthlessness that have weighted him down for so long.

Hypnosis is sometimes used as a means of going beyond the memory-conscious years of victims of ritual abuse.

86

While it can be harmful in some cases, hypnosis may bring them back to the time when this abuse was done to them. In many cases, it is important for them to realize that the physical abuse and evil burden came into their lives simultaneously, so they can understand the connection.

These victims usually go through a period of hatred and resentment because this abuse is often done by members of their own family or close friends of the family. While it is difficult for them to understand why this was done, it is beneficial for them to know that this is the source of their problem.

While pedophilia is beyond the scope of this book and has not been mentioned thus far, it should be noted that there is a distinct and important difference between pedophiliac acts and ritualistic abuse. In both cases, sexual aberrations are performed on children, but for different reasons. With pedophilia, sexual acts are done to small children so that the abuser may derive sexual pleasure. With ritualistic abuse, the harm is done so that the child will grow up believing he or she is evil. While the end result of sexual abuse is physically the same, with ritualistic abuse the victim has to carry the evil burden, discussed earlier in this book. The victim of pedophiliac acts is not made to carry this burden. In either case, however, the victim often blames himself for what happened to him and requires sometimes-extensive counseling to reverse this viewpoint and to rid himself of the shame and blame that he feels.

In counseling victims of any sort of sexual or ritualistic abuse, again I stress that there must be a constant repetition to the victims that they are not evil but that evil was done to them. They must be brought to the crystal clear realization that they did not do bad things, but that bad things were done to them.

Finally, when a person comes out of the darkness, it is vitally important that he be made to feel welcome in the church. He should be invited to join some church organization so he can feel more a part of the Kingdom of Light.

—The End—

For more information...

Believe The Children
P.O. Box 1358
Manhatan Beach, CA. 90266
(213) 379-3514
(213) 374-1648

Believe The Children
P.O. Box 840041
New Orleans, LA. 70124

Incest Survivors Anonymous
P.O. Box 5613
Long Beach, CA. 90805-0613
(213) 422-1632
(213) 428-5599

National Committee
For Prevention Of Child Abuse
2001 "O" St., N.W.
Washington, D.C. 20036
(202) 965-1900

Bothered About Dungeons & Dragons (BADD)
P.O. Box 5513
Richmond, VA. 23220
(804) 264-0403

Prayer to Saint Michael

Saint Michael, the Archangel,
defend us in battle.
Be our protection against the wickedness
and snares of the devil.
May God rebuke him, we humbly pray,
and do thou, O Prince of the Heavenly Host,
by the power of God, thrust into hell
Satan and all evil spirits
who wander through the world
for the ruin of souls.
Amen.

About the Author

FATHER JOSEPH F. BRENNAN is a parish priest in Lafayette, Louisiana. He is a counselor of children and adults who were ritualistically abused by Satanic cults. He also counsels people who are members of cults and who want to leave the cults to return to lives of spiritual normality.

A personal friend of Mother Teresa of Calcutta since 1977, Father Brennan does spiritual retreat work for Mother Teresa's Missionaries of Charity living in the United States, particularly in Lafayette, San Francisco and Washington, D.C.

He has been pastor of Saint Genevieve Catholic Church since 1982. Before that, he served as pastor or associate pastor in various Louisiana towns and cities, since 1959.

Father Brennan was ordained to the priesthood on May 7, 1959 after attending Saint John Seminary in Little Rock, Arkansas. He was director of the Cursillo Movement for the Catholic Diocese of Lafayette from 1974 to 1979.

He was born in Philadelphia, Pennsylvania, on Feb. 15, 1931, and was reared there.

Additional copies *of "The Kingdom of Darkness"
may be obtained by mail order for $11.95 plus $1.50 for
postage and handling, or $13.45 total. (Louisiana
residents add 90 cents tax.)*

*Send order, along with remittance to: Acadian House
Publishing, Box 52247, Lafayette, La. 70505.*

(Quantity discount schedule available upon request.)